A **CLOUD FOREST** Food Chain

A WHO-EATS-WHAT
Adventure in Africa

Rebecca Hogue Wojahn Donald Wojahn

Lerner Publications Company
Minneapolis

For Eli and Cal. We hope this answers some of your questions.

There are many links in the chain that created this series. Thanks to Ann Kerns, Kitty Creswell, Carol Hinz, Danielle Carnito, Sarah Olmanson, Paul Rodeen, the staff of the L. E. Phillips Memorial Public Library, and finally, Katherine Hogue

Lerner Publications Company
A division of Lerner Publishing Group, Inc.
241 First Avenue North
Minneapolis, MN 55401 U.S.A.

Website address: www.lernerbooks.com

Library of Congress Cataloging-in-Publication Data

Wojahn, Rebecca Hogue.
    A cloud forest food chain : a who-eats-what adventure in Africa / by Rebecca Hogue Wojahn and Donald Wojahn.
      p.   cm. — (Follow that food chain)
    Includes bibliographical references and index.
    ISBN 978-0-8225-7612-9 (lib. bdg. : alk. paper)
    1. Cloud forest ecology—Africa—Juvenile literature. 2. Food chains (Ecology) —Africa—Juvenile literature. I. Wojahn, Donald. II. Title.
QH194.W64 2010
577.34096—dc22   2008034090

Manufactured in the United States of America
1 2 3 4 5 6 – BP – 15 14 13 12 11 10

Contents

WELCOME TO AN
AFRICAN CLOUD FOREST . . . 4

CHOOSE A TERTIARY CONSUMER . . . 6

A CLOUD FOREST FOOD WEB . . . 31

TREES OF THE
AFRICAN CLOUD FOREST . . . 34

GLOSSARY . . . 60

FURTHER READING AND WEBSITES . . . 61

SELECTED BIBLIOGRAPHY . . . 62

INDEX . . . 63

Introduction
WELCOME TO AN AFRICAN CLOUD FOREST

The farther into the African cloud forest you get, the steeper the trail and the cooler and wetter the air. At night, temperatures can be near freezing. During the day, mist swirls in low spots. Those misty swirls give the cloud forest its name. A cloud forest is a type of **rain forest** that is high in the mountains. It's so high that it's almost always in the clouds.

Cloud forest trees are not as tall or as straight as trees in other rain forests. But cloud forest trees are thick. Moss coats their trunks. Vines hang down from the branches in tangles. The bushes grow so dense that you need to cut through them to go anywhere.

High above you in the trees, birds call and monkeys chatter to one another. Up ahead, something crashes through the brush. But it stays out of sight among the bamboo branches.

Cloud forests grow in the heart of Africa on mountains created by ancient volcanoes. These jungles are some of the last places on the planet to be explored by humans. Thousands of **species** of animals live in this **habitat**. Some species are not found anywhere else on Earth. Here you'll find humans' closest relatives—the great apes. Other species keep themselves so well hidden that few people have even seen them. Come meet just a few of them in this book.

AFRICA

N

Atlantic
Ocean

Indian
Ocean

■ **Cloud Forests**

The boxed area shows the cloud forests
of central Africa. This region includes
parts of Uganda, Rwanda, the Congo, and
the Ruwenzori Mountains.

Choose a
TERTIARY CONSUMER

All the living things in the African cloud forest are necessary for its health and survival. From the gorilla munching on a bamboo twig to the cockroach shuffling through the dead leaves, all living things are connected. Animals and other organisms feed on and transfer energy to one another. This is called a **food chain** or a **food web**.

In food chains, the strongest **predators** are called **tertiary consumers**. They hunt other animals for food and have few natural enemies. Some of the animals they eat are called **secondary consumers**. Secondary consumers are also predators. They hunt plant-eating animals. Plant eaters are **primary consumers**.

Plants are **producers**. Using energy from the sun, they produce their own food. Plants take in **nutrients** from the soil. They also provide nutrients to the animals that eat them.

Decomposers are insects or bacteria (tiny living things) that break down dead plants and animals. Decomposers change them into the nutrients found in the soil.

The plants and animals in a food chain depend on one another. Sometimes there's a break in the chain, such as one type of animal dying out. This loss ripples through the rest of the habitat.

Begin your journey through an African cloud forest food web by choosing a large **carnivore**, or meat eater. These tertiary consumers are at the top of the food chain. That means that, for the most part, they don't have any enemies in the cloud forest (except for humans).

When it's time for the tertiary consumer to eat, pick its meal and flip to that page. As you go through the book, don't be surprised if you backtrack and end up where you never expected to be. That's how food webs work—they're complicated. And watch out for those dead ends! When you hit one of those, you have to go back to page 7 and start over with another tertiary consumer.

The main role a plant or animal plays in the cloud forest food web is identified by a color-coded shape. Here is the key to that code:

TERTIARY CONSUMER

PRODUCER

SECONDARY CONSUMER

PRIMARY CONSUMER

DECOMPOSER

To choose . . .

. . . a leopard, TURN TO PAGE 8.
. . . an African golden cat, TURN TO PAGE 28.
. . . a black mamba snake, TURN TO PAGE 40.
. . . a martial eagle, TURN TO PAGE 49.

To learn more about a cloud forest food web, GO TO PAGE 31.

LEOPARD *(Panthera pardus)*

The young leopard cub shoots out of nowhere and pounces on a startled mouse. But the cub's hunting skills aren't very good. The mouse wiggles free. The leopard bats at the escaping mouse, but it ducks away.

The cub gives up this hunt. She looks up and spots the white tip of her mother's tail. She hustles over. Mom's got an African hare clenched in her jaws.

Leopards are not fussy eaters. They'll hunt animals as big as impalas and as tiny as insects. It all depends on what they can find and how hungry they are. A mother leopard especially can't afford to be choosy. Her cubs won't be ready to hunt for themselves until they are eighteen month old. She has to feed them and herself.

The cub mews in excitement. But just as the mother leopard sets the hare down, a honey badger comes growling out of the brush. He's hungry too, and he heads right for the dead hare. The mother leopard snarls back. She's worked hard for this catch, and her cubs need to eat.

But honey badgers are tough. This one isn't afraid of the mother leopard's claws or teeth. He grabs hold of the dead hare and tugs.

The cub tries to help out. The mother leopard gives up the hare and swats at her cub. She wants to protect her catch, but she is more concerned about keeping the cub safe. The honey badger might decide to snatch the cub instead of the dead hare. She pushes her cub up the tree. From the branches above, they watch the honey badger devour their dinner.

Yesterday's hunt went a little better. **Last night for dinner, the leopard cub gobbled down...**

Tiptoeing Hunters

The leopard is the Olympic athlete of the big cats. Leopards are good at running, leaping, and climbing. They are strong, fast, and smart, and can jump as no other cat can. All of these help them to capture a wide variety of prey. But their ability to stay quiet may be their best hunting skill. Leopards can sneak up on their prey by walking silently on their toes—much like you do when you tiptoe.

9

. . . an eastern black-and-white colobus monkey. To see what another eastern black-and-white colobus monkey is up to, TURN TO PAGE 32.

. . . an African golden cat cub. To see what another African golden cat is up to, TURN TO PAGE 28.

. . . a blue duiker. To see what another blue duiker is up to, TURN TO PAGE 58.

. . . an okapi. To see what another okapi is up to, TURN TO PAGE 24.

. . . a honey badger. To see what another honey badger is up to, TURN TO PAGE 37.

. . . a giant forest hog. To see what another giant forest hog is up to, TURN TO PAGE 16.

. . . speckled cockroaches. To see what another speckled cockroach is up to, TURN TO PAGE 14.

. . . a baby mountain gorilla. To see what another mountain gorilla is up to, TURN TO PAGE 18.

COLLARED SUNBIRD

(Anthreptes collaris)

The collared sunbird flits through the leaves high in the treetops. Up here it's like a garden in the air. The trees themselves sprout flowers. But thousands of other flowering plants grow here too. They hang from the trees and grow out of the cracks in the tree bark. Some of them are orchids and ferns. Others are long flowering vines called lianas and deep bowl-shaped plants called bromeliads. They all live here in the treetops. It's the best place to get the sunlight they need to grow.

And it's here that the sunbird zooms and rushes from flower to flower. At each bloom, he hovers for a moment, as hummingbirds do. He dips his long, curved beak into an orchid. His tongue is hollow like a drinking straw. He uses it to sip nectar out of the flower. The collared sunbird wouldn't be able to survive in the lower branches of the trees. There just aren't enough flowers down below. And the flowers need him too. Each visit of his spreads the flowers' pollen—the powdery substance that helps new flowers grow.

Zip! There he goes again. Did you miss him? That's not surprising. Despite his brilliant coloring, he's almost impossible to see. He's just too quick and too small.

Last night for dinner, the collared sunbird gulped down . . .

. . . more nectar from flowers in the trees. To read about the trees of the forest, **TURN TO PAGE 34.**

. . . a butterfly caterpillar. To find out what another butterfly is up to, **TURN TO PAGE 27.**

. . . a speckled cockroach. To find out what another speckled cockroach is up to, **TURN TO PAGE 14.**

ROCK HYRAX *(Procavia capensis)*

The hyrax uncurls herself from around her babies. Around her, the rest of the group begins to stir too. They are all tightly packed together in a crevice (large crack) in the rock they call home. Huddling together is the only way these small, furry animals can keep warm when the air is cool. The hyrax has extra long hairs all over her body. She uses them to feel her way out of the dark crevice.

The hyrax and her group stretch out in the sun to warm up. After sunbathing, the group spreads out to nibble on nearby plants and flowers. The hyrax bends and rips a leaf off with her back teeth. Hyraxes have sharp tusks—teeth that stick out of their mouths. But the hyraxes only use their tusks to defend themselves. They use their rear teeth for eating.

On the stone above them, the male of the group keeps an eye out for trouble. *Squeak*! He spots something. Instantly, the mother and her babies run for cover. She scrambles straight up the face of the wall. Her feet start sweating when she runs. This makes them sticky so she can climb. Yes, that's right, sweaty feet make the hyrax a good climber!

She huddles again with her babies, waiting for the all-clear signal. Then she goes back to eating. *Yesterday, she nibbled . . .*

Big Relatives

Hyraxes look a little like giant guinea pigs or rabbits. But some researchers believe that hyraxes are actually related to elephants. Millions of years ago, it's possible that both hyraxes and elephants came from the same prehistoric animals. In fact, millions of years ago, hyraxes were the size of oxen. That would explain why the skulls and feet of modern hyraxes and elephants are very similar. It also explains why hyraxes have mini-tusks.

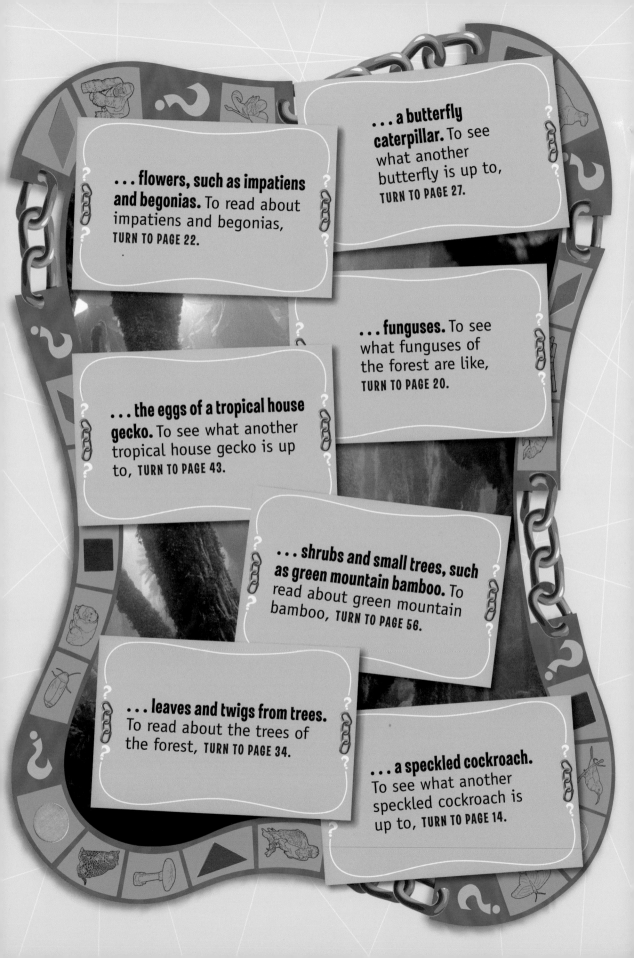

. . . a butterfly caterpillar. To see what another butterfly is up to, TURN TO PAGE 27.

. . . flowers, such as impatiens and begonias. To read about impatiens and begonias, TURN TO PAGE 22.

. . . funguses. To see what funguses of the forest are like, TURN TO PAGE 20.

. . . the eggs of a tropical house gecko. To see what another tropical house gecko is up to, TURN TO PAGE 43.

. . . shrubs and small trees, such as green mountain bamboo. To read about green mountain bamboo, TURN TO PAGE 56.

. . . leaves and twigs from trees. To read about the trees of the forest, TURN TO PAGE 34.

. . . a speckled cockroach. To see what another speckled cockroach is up to, TURN TO PAGE 14.

SPECKLED COCKROACH *(Nauphoeta cinerea)*

Under the cover of fallen leaves, the speckled cockroach chews through some wet, slimy, old vegetation. As a decomposer, she is helping to break down the dead plants and **decomposing** dead animals of the forest. Whoops! Suddenly, the air is bright and cool. A giant forest hog digging for roots has stirred up the ground. Now the speckled cockroach is out in the open. She scuttles back under the layer of dead leaves where it is safe and dark.

Her cockroach friends have left fluids from their bodies behind on the ground as they move along. She follows these chemical trails to find the other cockroaches. Cockroaches don't really organize into groups. But they do prefer to cluster together. She finds and settles in with several others at the base of a camphor tree.

Partway through the night, she stops eating. A little later, she lays an egg case—a batch of eggs held together by a thin skin. Inside the case are thirty tiny eggs. Baby cockroaches will hatch out of the egg case. At this stage, the young insects are called larvas. For their first meal, the larvas eat the egg case. After filling themselves, they crawl under and aboard their mother. Some even snuggle under her wings.

As the sun rises in the morning, the speckled cockroach with her new larvas burrows a little deeper beneath the ground cover. They'll rest until morning.

Last night for dinner, the speckled cockroach chewed on . . .

The Ultimate Survivor

A common joke says that if a nuclear war ever happens, only cockroaches will survive. But joking aside, cockroaches are some of the most flexible and toughest creatures on Earth. Cockroaches have been around for millions of years. Thousands of cockroach species exist all over the world. Many species can go a month without food. Some can go forty-five minutes without air. And some can live even if their heads are nipped off!

. . . **wilted flowers, such as impatiens and begonias.** To read about impatiens and begonias, TURN TO PAGE 22.

. . . **a dead swallowtail butterfly.** To see what another butterfly is up to, TURN TO PAGE 27.

. . . **rotten fruit and leaves from trees.** To read about the trees of the forest, TURN TO PAGE 34.

. . . **a termite nest.** To see what some termites are up to, TURN TO PAGE 47.

. . . **mushrooms and other funguses.** To read about the funguses of the forest, TURN TO PAGE 20.

. . . **a dead chimpanzee.** To see what another chimpanzee is up to, TURN TO PAGE 44.

. . . **dead green mountain bamboo.** To read about green mountain bamboo, TURN TO PAGE 56.

GIANT FOREST HOG *(Hylochoerus meinertzhageni)*

The giant forest hog grunts, and her piglets come running. They duck beneath her round hairy belly for safety. Nearby, two males are wrestling. They don't notice anyone around them. And at 660 pounds (299 kilograms) and more than 6 feet (2 meters) long, they could trample a piglet by accident. The mother shuffles her babies a safe distance away.

The two males run at each other. They push at each other's faces. Each is trying to push the other off balance. The warty growth behind their eyes protects the eyes from getting sliced open by the other's tusks (long teeth). With one bash, their foreheads meet straight on. A loud crack echoes through the forest. The younger male staggers a little. He stops and pants. He shakes his head to clear it. After a few more breaths, he gives up and turns away. The older male has won the fight. That means he is still in charge of this sounder, or group of hogs.

Now that the battle is over, the mother hog starts digging in the dirt again with her foot-long (0.3 m) side tusks. Her babies timidly peek out from under her belly. When they see she is eating again, they tumble out into the open. They push one another out of the way to get at the food their mother is digging up.

Last night for dinner, the giant forest hog gobbled down . . .

. . . flowers, such as impatiens and begonias. To read about impatiens and begonias, TURN TO PAGE 22.

. . . mushrooms and other funguses. To read about the funguses of the forest, TURN TO PAGE 20.

. . . green mountain bamboo. To read about green mountain bamboo, TURN TO PAGE 56.

. . . fruit and leaves from trees. To read about the trees of the forest, TURN TO PAGE 34.

MOUNTAIN GORILLA *(Gorilla beringei beringei)*

The mountain gorilla rolls over, trying to go back to sleep. But it's no use. Her baby is tickling her ear with a flower. She swats at him playfully and then stretches and gets up.

Her baby is delighted. Time to go out and find some food! The mother plucks some leaves from a bush and chews slowly. Her baby watches and then copies her.

Around them their family group is waking up. They're rising out of the nests they built last night. Each evening the gorillas break off branches from bushes and trees to form cozy nests on the ground for sleeping.

The baby sees a friend and leaps up. He just started walking a few weeks ago when he turned five months old. Now he skips along on his back legs, balancing himself with the knuckles of his front legs.

Whoops! He trips over his own feet and tumbles into the largest gorilla of the group. This gorilla is enormous. He weighs more than 500 pounds (230 kilograms). Shaggy, black fur grows on his head, arms, and legs. His back glints with silver fur.

This gorilla is called a silverback. He's the leader of the group. He's also the baby's father. But that doesn't mean the baby gorilla can bother him anytime he wants. The silverback snorts and wheels around to face the baby.

It's just a "cough grunt"—a warning for the baby to mind his manners. Still, it frightens the baby. He squawks and tears back to his mother. She holds him in her lap until he starts to squirm impatiently again. A butterfly flutters overhead, and he reaches out to it. The mother gorilla gives him a squeeze and lets him go. She knows that the family group will all help keep him safe.

But the group's protection isn't always enough. Two out of every five baby gorillas die within their first year. Some get sick, some are caught by predators, and some get killed by people.

Mountain gorillas are some of the rarest animals on the planet. They have been protected by law since 1933. Yet every year, some are killed by **poachers**—people who hunt animals illegally. Other gorillas find their homes broken up as the forest is cut down. There are fewer than seven hundred left in the wild. Many people expect them to become **extinct** unless we take drastic action to save the cloud forest environment. Without action, the baby gorilla, his mother, and the silverback are **endangered**. They are a *DEAD END*.

19

FUNGUS

The damp, dark floor of the African cloud forest is full of dead leaves, rotten logs and spoiled fruit and flowers. Growing off these dead things are the spongy funguses of the forest—mushrooms, toadstools, yeast, and molds. Some fungus is big enough for animals and people to harvest as food. But much of it is too small for the human eye to see.

All kinds of funguses are crucial for the life of the forest. Funguses break down dead material—dead plants and the **decomposing** bodies of dead animals. This broken-down material is full of nutrients that mix into the soil. Without funguses, the forest floor would be stacked high with dead leaves and broken sticks. And the dirt itself would have fewer of the nutrients that plants need to grow.

Last night for dinner, the funguses of the forest grew off...

. . . a termite nest. To see what other termites are up to, TURN TO PAGE 47.

. . . a dead African golden cat. To see what another African golden cat is up to, TURN TO PAGE 28.

. . . wilted flowers, such as impatiens and begonias. To read about impatiens and begonias, TURN TO PAGE 22.

. . . a dead leopard. To see what another leopard is up to, TURN TO PAGE 8.

. . . rotten fruit and leaves from trees. To read about the trees of the forest, TURN TO PAGE 34.

. . . dead green mountain bamboo. To read about green mountain bamboo, TURN TO PAGE 56.

. . . a dead martial eagle. To see what another martial eagle is up to, TURN TO PAGE 49.

. . . a dead chimpanzee. To see what another chimpanzee is up to, TURN TO PAGE 44.

IMPATIENS AND BEGONIAS

Above: Impatiens
Below: Begonias

Most flowers in the cloud forest grow up high in the trees where the sunlight hits. But some, such as impatiens and begonias, love the shade, moisture, and coolness of the forest floor. Down here they spread far and wide in pink, red, white, and yellow blankets over the ground.

If you ask a gardener, he or she is probably familiar with impatiens and begonias. These are some of the most popular flowers to grow in gardens around the world. Chances are good that some are growing right in your neighborhood.

The impatiens and begonias soak up the nutrients in the soil left behind by decomposers and the **decomposing** bodies of dead animals. *Last night for dinner, the trees soaked up nutrients from . . .*

. . . **a dead Ruwenzori turaco.** To see what another Ruwenzori turaco is up to, **TURN TO PAGE 52.**

. . . **termites.** To see what other termites are up to, **TURN TO PAGE 47.**

. . . **a dead leopard.** To see what another leopard is up to, **TURN TO PAGE 8.**

. . . **a dead collared sunbird.** To see what another collared sunbird is up to, **TURN TO PAGE 11.**

. . . **a dead black mamba.** To see what another black mamba is up to, **TURN TO PAGE 40.**

. . . **a dead tropical house gecko.** To see what another tropical house gecko is up to, **TURN TO PAGE 43.**

. . . **a dead martial eagle.** To see what another martial eagle is up to, **TURN TO PAGE 49.**

OKAPI *(Okapi johnstoni)*

The okapi wraps his long, black tongue around a branch. With a tug, his tongue pulls off all the leaves and stashes them in his mouth. After a few chomps, he sticks his tongue out again. It stretches to almost 1 foot (0.3 meters). If he wanted to, he could lick his eyes and clean out his own ears with his tongue. He is a close relative of the giraffe, which also has an extra-long tongue for grabbing things.

The okapi picks his way along the forest trail. Under his hooves are scent glands. As he walks, he leaves behind a tarlike substance that marks this as his area.

But what's this? His huge ears twitch at a sound. A cry in the forest. He recognizes it as the sound of another okapi. He trots forward to see who has invaded his territory. As he presses his way through the brush, he stops at the edge of a deep pit. Local people have dug it to catch their dinner. At the bottom of the hole, a young female okapi lies curled up. The two make chuffing noises as a greeting, but there's nothing the male can do to help her out. He continues on, looking for his next bite of leaves.

Last night for dinner, the okapi chewed on . . .

Can't Tell a Zebra by Its Stripes

Okapis were once thought to be extinct. That's because only their fossilized remains from millions of years ago were ever seen. Then in the late 1880s and early 1900s, a rumor spread among Europeans in Africa of a "forest zebra." (Can you guess how this rumor got started? Think of the striped back end of the okapi.) Finally, in 1901, local Africans showed a hide (animal skin) and two skulls to Europeans. The Europeans discovered that this "new" animal was not a zebra at all. It was the modern-day okapi.

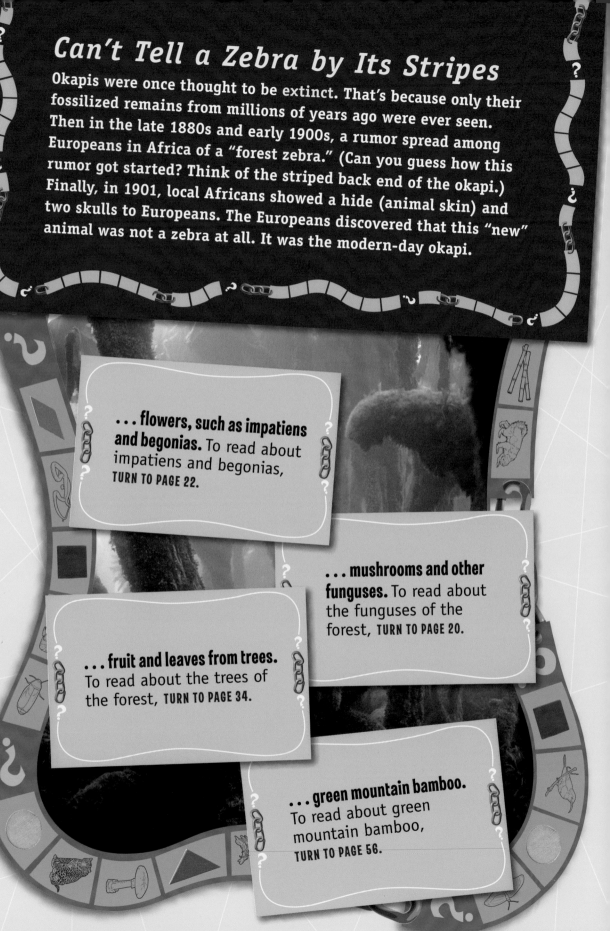

. . . **flowers, such as impatiens and begonias.** To read about impatiens and begonias, **TURN TO PAGE 22.**

. . . **mushrooms and other funguses.** To read about the funguses of the forest, **TURN TO PAGE 20.**

. . . **fruit and leaves from trees.** To read about the trees of the forest, **TURN TO PAGE 34.**

. . . **green mountain bamboo.** To read about green mountain bamboo, **TURN TO PAGE 56.**

HIGHLAND MANGABEY *(Rungwecebus kipunji)*

Uh-oh, this is a **DEAD END**. The highland mangabey, also called a kipunji, is very **endangered**. This light brown, fluffy monkey was first spotted in the mountains of Africa by scientists in 2005. But as soon as the discovery was announced, the highland mangabey was listed as in danger of becoming **extinct**. Scientists guess there are probably fewer than one thousand left. Humans are destroying the highland mangabey's habitat. People cut down trees in the area for lumber and land. What's left of the cloud forest habitat is divided up by towns and farms. This makes it hard for different bands of monkeys to find one another. This rich, diverse cloud forest habitat might be the home to other species we don't even know about. They could disappear before humans get a chance to learn about them.

BUTTERFLIES
(Lepidoptera)

The butterfly zigzags up on the breeze near the tops of the trees. He flutters, stopping by a bloom or two to take a sip of nectar with his curly tongue.

After he drinks his fill, he follows other butterflies down to a clearing. Here the sun is breaking through the shade and mist. The butterflies stay in the sun, drifting toward the clearing. Now the clearing widens. Only stumps remain where towering trees once stood. The butterfly alights on a stump for a moment. Then he joins other butterflies—swallowtails, swordtails, diadems, and many more—sunning themselves on a wide strip of warm, bare dirt. He lands on the smooth ground, pumping his wings and soaking in the sun.

Suddenly, a rumble shakes the ground under him. Before he knows it, a jeep zooms over the hill. The butterflies scatter, but they are sucked into the fast-moving vehicle. Our butterfly is whipped up in the air in the wind created by the jeep. He spins, out of control, to the side of the road. He lands in some tall grass.

Slowly, he checks his wings. He takes a test flight. Everything still seems to work. He's one of the lucky ones.

Last night for dinner, the butterfly drank nectar from . . .

. . . **flowers, such as impatiens and begonias.** To read about impatiens and begonias, **TURN TO PAGE 22.**

. . . **fruit and leaves from trees.** To read about the trees of the forest, **TURN TO PAGE 34.**

AFRICAN GOLDEN CAT *(Felis aurata)*

As the day darkens, the African golden cat stretches her front legs out on a tree limb. She's twice as big as a pet cat. In the shadows, it's nearly impossible to see her reddish brown body as she slinks down the tree trunk. Her ability to hide is part of what makes her such a successful hunter.

She reaches the bottom of the tree and pads off into the dusk. Frogs croak and birds call around her. Most don't even know she's within earshot. She stalks through the thick leaves and brush.

Her ears perk up. What's that? The golden cat watches as a crowned eagle flaps to the ground in the clearing right in front of her. A still-squirming squirrel is tight in the eagle's talons.

Dinner is served! The African golden cat pushes through the leaves of the bush. With a leap, she springs onto the eagle and the squirrel. One swipe with her heavy paw and sharp claws sends the eagle flapping away. She grabs the squirrel and bites down. It's not often that dinner is delivered right to her.

Last night for dinner, the African golden cat pounced and ate . . .

Mystery Cat

African golden cats are very good at hiding and keeping private. That means that animal scientists have a hard time learning about them. For example, no one knows how many kittens they usually have or how the kittens are cared for. An African golden cat den has never been found or studied in the wild. African golden cats are one of the secrets of the misty mountain forests.

. . . a collared sunbird in its nest. To see what another collared sunbird is up to, TURN TO PAGE 11.

. . . a rock hyrax. To see what another rock hyrax is up to, TURN TO PAGE 12.

. . . a Ruwenzori turaco. To see what another Ruwenzori turaco is up to, TURN TO PAGE 52.

. . . a giant otter shrew. To see what another giant otter shrew is up to, TURN TO PAGE 54.

. . . a couple of tropical house geckos. To see what another tropical house gecko is up to, TURN TO PAGE 43.

. . . a blue duiker. To see what another blue duiker is up to, TURN TO PAGE 58.

. . . a honey badger. To see what another honey badger is up to, TURN TO PAGE 37.

. . . an infant highland mangabey. To see what another highland mangabey is up to, TURN TO PAGE 26.

STRANGE-HORNED CHAMELEON

(Bradypodion xenorhinia)

Do you see that strange-horned chameleon resting on the branch of that ficus tree? No? Well, he was there a minute ago.

Too bad you missed him, because you may never come near another. Strange-horned chameleons are incredibly rare. They are found only in the Ruwenzori Mountains of Africa. There used to be more, but people loved watching these chameleons with the funny-looking circular bump on their noses. Too many were taken from the mountains as pets or for zoos. Now hardly anyone gets to see them at all. That's right—this is a **DEAD END** for animals looking to munch on a strange-horned chameleon.

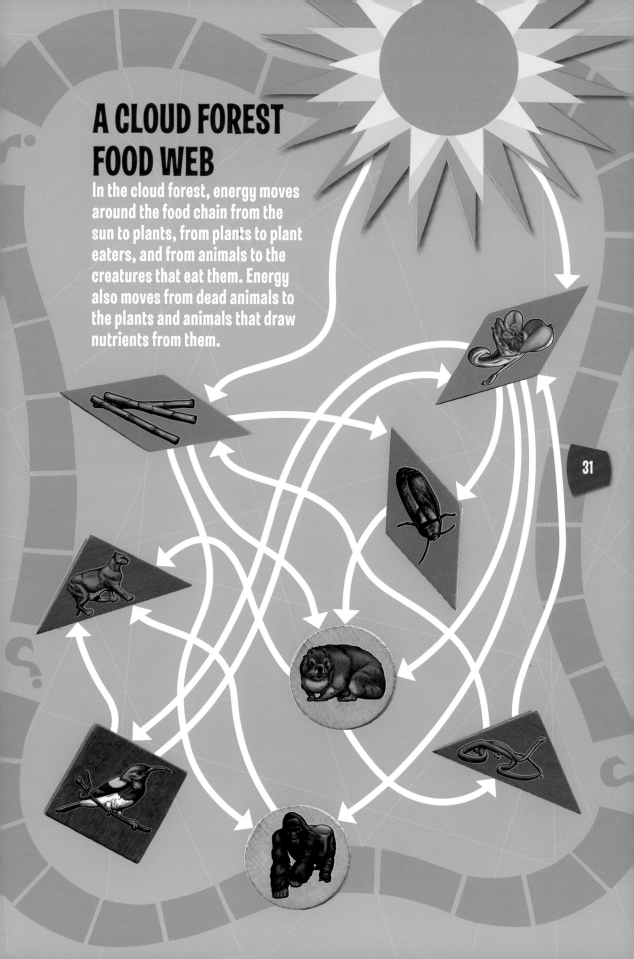

A CLOUD FOREST FOOD WEB

In the cloud forest, energy moves around the food chain from the sun to plants, from plants to plant eaters, and from animals to the creatures that eat them. Energy also moves from dead animals to the plants and animals that draw nutrients from them.

EASTERN BLACK-AND-WHITE COLOBUS
(Colobus guereza)

The eastern black-and-white colobus monkey grabs a branch. He swings his body through the air and stretches his other arm out to catch the next branch. This method of swinging through the rain forest is called **brachiating**. It looks exactly like what you do at the playground on the monkey bars. But a colobus monkey can do it with his feet too. Brachiating is one of the fastest ways for him to get around.

The monkey settles in the crook of a tree. Around him are the female monkeys and babies of the group. They groom, play, and eat while he nibbles on a piece of fruit. He's also scanning the area. He's always on the lookout for any predators that might threaten his family group.

He sits up. What's that shadow down below? It's hard to tell in the dappled sunlight. Oh, no! It's the spotted coat of a hungry leopard! With a scream, he flings his fruit at this predator. He keeps yelling. His cries are very loud because of the extra-large voice box in his throat.

Instantly, his family group springs into action. His calls tell them which way to go. They flee up the trees, to where the branches can't support the heavy leopard. For now, the monkeys are safe.

The eastern black-and-white colobus monkey has escaped becoming a leopard meal. But as the day goes on, he must think about his own food. *Last night for dinner he tasted . . .*

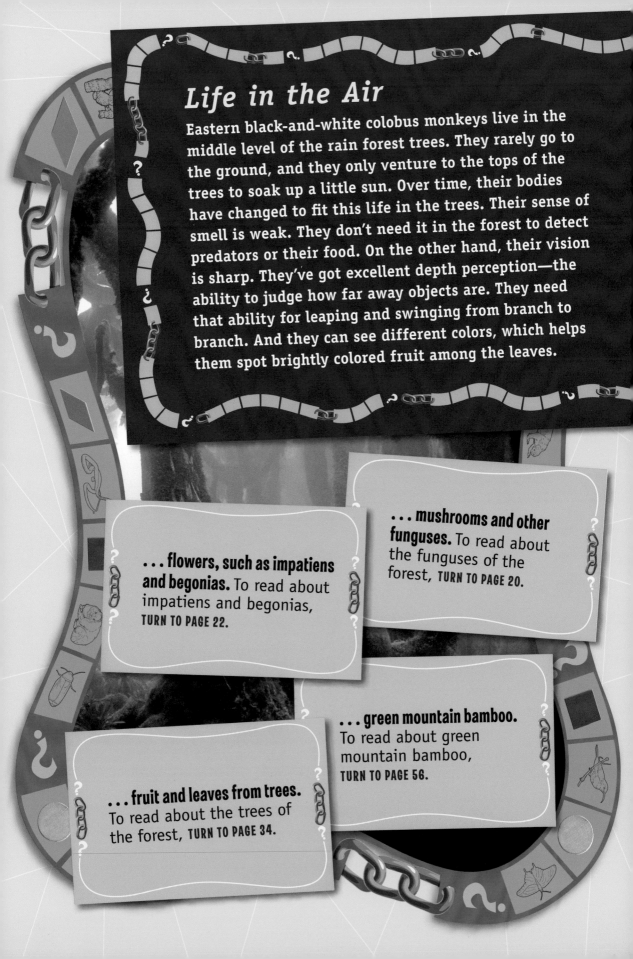

Life in the Air

Eastern black-and-white colobus monkeys live in the middle level of the rain forest trees. They rarely go to the ground, and they only venture to the tops of the trees to soak up a little sun. Over time, their bodies have changed to fit this life in the trees. Their sense of smell is weak. They don't need it in the forest to detect predators or their food. On the other hand, their vision is sharp. They've got excellent depth perception—the ability to judge how far away objects are. They need that ability for leaping and swinging from branch to branch. And they can see different colors, which helps them spot brightly colored fruit among the leaves.

. . . flowers, such as impatiens and begonias. To read about impatiens and begonias, TURN TO PAGE 22.

. . . mushrooms and other funguses. To read about the funguses of the forest, TURN TO PAGE 20.

. . . green mountain bamboo. To read about green mountain bamboo, TURN TO PAGE 56.

. . . fruit and leaves from trees. To read about the trees of the forest, TURN TO PAGE 34.

TREES OF THE AFRICAN CLOUD FOREST

The tree trunks of the African cloud forest stretch out of the bushes and shrubs. Mosses and lichens blanket them in green. Hanging ferns and **epiphytes** (plants that don't need soil to grow) drape the trees. At the very top of the forest, the trees burst wide in crowns of branches, leaves, and flowers. Up here, they soak in the sun and weave together to form the **canopy**.

The floor of the cloud forest

But more and more often, people cut down these trees. They cut them down for lumber or to clear the way for roads or farms. When the trees are cleared, the creatures that depend on them for food and shelter are never the same.

The trees' roots soak up the nutrients in the soil left behind by decomposers and the **decomposing** bodies of dead animals. *Last night for dinner, the trees soaked up nutrients from . . .*

Plants make food and oxygen through photosynthesis. Plants draw in carbon dioxide (a gas found in air) and water. Then they use the energy from sunlight to turn the carbon dioxide and water into their food.

Clouds rest over the trees in Bwindi National Park in Uganda.

35

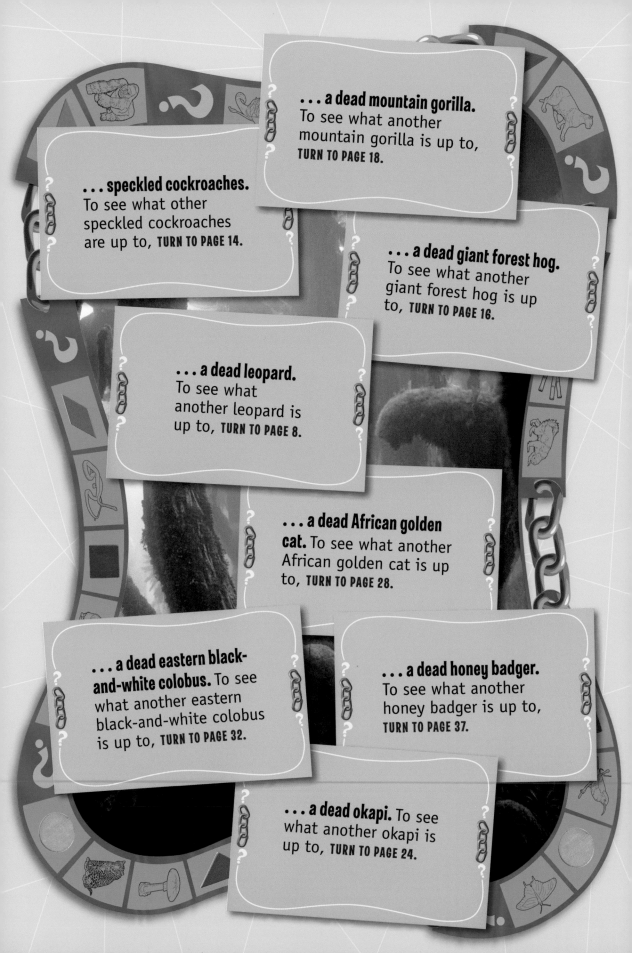

... a dead mountain gorilla. To see what another mountain gorilla is up to, **TURN TO PAGE 18.**

... speckled cockroaches. To see what other speckled cockroaches are up to, **TURN TO PAGE 14.**

... a dead giant forest hog. To see what another giant forest hog is up to, **TURN TO PAGE 16.**

... a dead leopard. To see what another leopard is up to, **TURN TO PAGE 8.**

... a dead African golden cat. To see what another African golden cat is up to, **TURN TO PAGE 28.**

... a dead eastern black-and-white colobus. To see what another eastern black-and-white colobus is up to, **TURN TO PAGE 32.**

... a dead honey badger. To see what another honey badger is up to, **TURN TO PAGE 37.**

... a dead okapi. To see what another okapi is up to, **TURN TO PAGE 24.**

HONEY BADGER *(Mellivora capensis)*

A honey badger carries a piece of honeycomb.

The honey badger rips apart a beehive. Angry bees buzz around his head. Honey drips from his mouth and his long, sharp claws. The hive is ripped apart. Already birds are cautiously approaching, hoping to clean up the dead bees. But they'll wait until the honey badger leaves.

The honey badger pauses in his destruction of a beehive. He has heard the cry of a tree hyrax in trouble. Well, his work here is finished. He sets out to see what is going on. In a clearing, he creeps up on a puff adder snake and the tree hyrax he heard. The puff adder is just pulling its long fangs from the hyrax's body. The snake watches and waits as its **venom** (poison) starts to work on the twitching hyrax.

The honey badger doesn't wait. This looks like a prime opportunity for a meaty meal to go with his honey. He charges in and snatches the hyrax in his powerful jaws. The snake hisses and rears up. It's not about to give up this meal!

Record-Holder

For years, honey badgers have been listed as the most fearless animal in the world in the *Guinness World Records*. A honey badger will attack just about any animal, even if it's poisonous or bigger than itself. Their sharp teeth and long claws, meant for digging, are great weapons. They also have tough, loose skin that makes it hard for other animals to hurt them in a fight.

But the badger is quicker than the snake. He hauls the hyrax behind a tree. In just a couple of gulps, the hyrax is history.

But the honey badger is still hungry. Where did that puff adder go anyway? The honey badger retraces his steps. He finds the snake sunning itself on a log not far away. As the badger approaches, the snake slides off the log and tries to escape. But the badger doesn't hesitate. He bites the back of the snake's head with his strong teeth. The snake writhes and twists. The badger loses his hold for just a split second. It's just long enough for the snake to twist and pierce the badger's tough skin with its fangs. Venom pumps into the badger. The badger bites the snake again and kills it.

But the venom is starting to numb the badger. In minutes he is on the ground next to the dead snake. His body is swollen and unable to move. But, unlike the snake, the badger is still alive. In a few hours, the venom will wear off. And the badger will finally chomp down the snake, the third part of his meal.

Last night for dinner, the honey badger chowed down on . . .

. . . mushrooms and other funguses. To read about the funguses of the forest, TURN TO PAGE 20.

. . . a speckled cockroach. To see what another speckled cockroach is up to, TURN TO PAGE 14.

. . . a giant otter shrew. To see what another giant otter shrew is up to, TURN TO PAGE 54.

. . . termites. To see what other termites are up to, TURN TO PAGE 47.

. . . a collared sunbird. To see what another collared sunbird is up to, TURN TO PAGE 11.

. . . a black mamba. To see what another black mamba is up to, TURN TO PAGE 40.

. . . a butterfly. To see what another butterfly is up to, TURN TO PAGE 27.

. . . a rock hyrax. To see what another rock hyrax is up to, TURN TO PAGE 12.

BLACK MAMBA *(Dendroaspis polyleptis)*

The warm air of morning pours in through the entrance to the black mamba's den. The snake slowly uncoils himself—all 8 feet (2.4 meters). He slithers out of the abandoned termite mound he calls home. Then he winds his way to a nearby rock. His movements are slow because it's been a cold night. He'll bask on the rock to get warm again.

Most black mambas aren't really black. Their skin is olive green, gray, or brownish gray. "Black" refers to the color of the inside of their mouths.

Hours later, he starts flicking his tongue. Each time he moves it in and out of his mouth, he brings smells to an organ in the back of his throat. Suddenly, he catches the scent of a female black mamba. He raises his head and slides off the rock in search of her. She will make a good mate.

The snake follows the female's scent trail. It runs along an antelope path in the forest. As he turns a corner, he runs into another black mamba male. This snake is also tracking down the female. She will mate with the one that finds her first.

Beware of Mambas

Black mambas are one of the fastest and the most deadly snakes in the world. If you come across a black mamba, back away slowly. You can't outrun them. They speed along at over 12 miles (19 kilometers) an hour. And if it strikes you with its fangs, you are in trouble. Its venom can kill a person in just twenty minutes. An antivenom medicine exists. But this cure for snake poison only helps victims that get a dose of the medicine in time.

As soon as they meet, the two male snakes raise their heads high. They bob at each other. Then the first black mamba loops his body around the stranger's. In seconds the two are twisted up together as tight as a piece of rope.

The two snakes roll around on the path. Their bodies are kinked and twisted, but their heads are raised high. Each is trying to wrestle the other's head down. They roll and coil for hours.

Finally, the first black mamba wraps his tail around the stranger in one more twist. Exhausted, the stranger's head sinks into the leaves. The two snakes unwrap themselves. The stranger slinks back into the forest. The victorious black mamba rests for a moment. Then he continues on the female's scent trail.

Finally, he finds her. She holds still. He flicks his tongue over the length of her body, and they mate.

After, he slips off back into the brush. An unlucky rock hyrax stumbles in his path. In a flash, he rears and strikes with his fangs. The fangs are filled with **venom**—a poison. The venom paralyses the hyrax in just moments. Then the mamba slowly swallows the hyrax whole. Lumpy with his full meal, he heads back to his termite den.

Meanwhile, the female mamba heads back to her underground den in a nearby rock crevice. Two months from now, she'll lay fourteen eggs in the den. She'll protect the eggs, but once the baby snakes hatch, they are on their own. They will live and hunt alone—just as their mother and father do.

Last night, the black mamba swallowed . . .

41

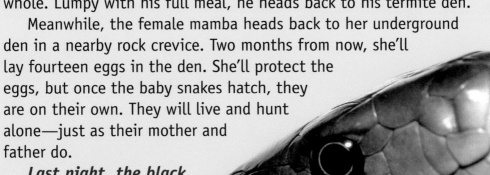

. . . **a martial eagle egg.** To see what another martial eagle is up to, TURN TO PAGE 49.

. . . **an infant highland mangabey.** To see what another highland mangabey is up to, TURN TO PAGE 26.

. . . **a rock hyrax.** To see what another rock hyrax is up to, TURN TO PAGE 12.

. . . **Ruwenzori turaco eggs.** To see what another Ruwenzori turaco is up to, TURN TO PAGE 52.

. . . **an eastern black-and-white colobus monkey.** To see what another eastern black-and-white colobus monkey is up to, TURN TO PAGE 32.

. . . **a tropical house gecko.** To see what another tropical house gecko is up to, TURN TO PAGE 43.

. . . **a blue duiker.** To see what another blue duiker is up to, TURN TO PAGE 58.

. . . **a strange-horned chameleon.** To see what another strange-horned chameleon is up to, TURN TO PAGE 30.

TROPICAL HOUSE GECKO *(Hemidactylus mabouia)*

Chirp, chirp. No, that's not a cricket or a bird. It's a tropical house gecko, calling out in the night. Geckos are the only lizards in the world that make this kind of call.

This gecko steals out into the night, inching up the trunk of the tree. His grayish green, rough body blends in perfectly on the bumpy tree bark. He takes a minute to clean his eyes. He doesn't have eyelids. Instead, a clear, thin skin protects his eyes. He carefully wipes the skin clean with his tongue. Now that he can see clearly, he grabs a tiny moth from midair. *Crunch, crunch.*

The gecko continues up the tree until he reaches a branch. He doesn't bother to climb onto the top side of it. He just keeps walking upside down on the bottom side. He has tiny bristles on the bottom of each of his toes to help him cling to the branch. The bristles create a suction that helps the gecko walk up vertical surfaces as well as upside down. The gecko's toes even bend backward. This lets him peel his toes off surfaces when needed.

Last night for dinner, the tropical house gecko snacked on . . .

43

. . . a butterfly. To see what another butterfly is up to, TURN TO PAGE 27.

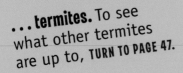**. . . termites.** To see what other termites are up to, TURN TO PAGE 47.

. . . a speckled cockroach. To see what another speckled cockroach is up to, TURN TO PAGE 14.

CHIMPANZEE *(Pan troglodytes)*

The young chimpanzee finishes his morning snack of roots and leaves. Then he climbs aboard a female's back. She snuggles him in tight. His mother was killed last year, but this female from the **troop** adopted him. She cares for him as if he were her own baby. He clings to her, enjoying the piggyback ride.

When the chimpanzee troop gets to a clearing, he tumbles off her. She grabs him before he can dash off. He holds still for a minute while she grooms him. She picks burrs, bugs, and mites from his fur. Then she gives him a quick nuzzle and off he goes to join the other youngsters of the troop.

They are sitting around a termite hill. He squeals in delight. He knows this trick! He grabs a twig and rams it into a hole. After a few seconds, he pulls it out. The end of the stick wriggles with termites. Yum! It's a termite lollypop! He slurps them off and sticks the twig back in for second helpings.

But before he can pull it out again, he's startled by a shrill sound. The leader of the band, an old male, has screeched out a warning.

The young chimpanzee frantically looks for his adopted mom. The older male hoots and hollers. His fur stands on end. He swings his arms and throws sticks at the edge of the clearing. Others join in.

The young chimp finds his mother and hides on her back. Peering around her shoulder, he sees several humans approaching through the trees. His mother and the rest of the females and babies flee through the forest.

44

Our Closest Relatives

Of all the animals in the world, humans are most like chimpanzees. Just a tiny bit of our genetic material is different. We are so closely related to chimpanzees, that if we needed to, we could use chimpanzee blood in our bodies. Because we are so similar, the germs that make chimpanzees sick can also make humans sick. In fact, some of our most deadly diseases, such as AIDS and Ebola, have come from chimpanzees.

45

Unfortunately, this is a **DEAD END**. Although this young chimp and his mother escape, many of the troop don't. Those people coming through the trees are **poachers**—people who hunt animals illegally. Poachers are one of the reasons that chimpanzees are in danger of becoming **extinct**. Poachers capture baby chimps for zoos and as pets. But the adults in the chimpanzee troop will stand and protect their young. Poachers just shoot the adults to get them out of the way. For every baby that is taken, an average of ten adult chimpanzees are killed.

Chimps are also **endangered** because of loss of habitat. When the forests get cut down for roads and cities, it leaves open spaces between stands of trees. Female chimpanzees, out looking for mates, won't cross these treeless spaces. That means they have a hard time connecting with new chimpanzee communities. And when they don't meet new mates from other communities, they stay and mate with males in their own troops. The babies from these chimpanzees are often weaker, more likely to get sick, and don't survive. This has become such a problem that the government of the African country Uganda began planting trees to reconnect the chimpanzee communities.

TERMITES *(Macrotermes vitrialatus)*

Drip, drip, drip. The rain patters down through the trees of the forest. It hits a funny-shaped tower of hardened dirt. The tower is a few feet high. At its top is a mushroomlike cap, with another cap on top of that. This is a termite mound. The fancy cap works like an umbrella. It keeps the forest's rain from flooding the termite **colony** and nest below.

As the rain splashes off the tower, some termites start to crawl out of it. These aren't the usual blind, flightless termites seen working around the forest. These termites have eyes and wings. In moments the termites take flight. All around the clearing, termites fly from their nests.

These termites are called alates—the kings and queens of future colonies. They fly clumsily through the air, looking for mates. When two alates make a match, the pair settles back on the ground. They find a beetle hole and crawl into it. It will become their royal chamber. Soon, the queen will lay eggs—up to thirty thousand a day. The royal couple's children will become a new colony of worker and soldier termites. They will take care of the king and queen in a new nest.

A winged alate termite

While the alates look for mates, the colony's worker termites are busy. They are chewing up the dead wood of the cloud forest for their king and queen. This will help to feed their colony. Also, as decomposers, the termites help break down the forest so that other plants and animals can use its nutrients.

Last night for dinner, the termites chewed on . . .

Insect Royalty

The queen and king will never leave their colony again. They'll remain at the center of the nest until they die. The queen is the true ruler. She gives directions to the colony through scents she gives off from her enormous body. One of the workers' jobs is to lick her clean. When the workers do, they get her scent message. This message is then carried to the rest of the colony and delivered through the colony's food. Queen termites can rule up to twenty years!

... **flowers, such as impatiens and begonias.** To read about impatiens and begonias, TURN TO PAGE 22.

... **mushrooms and other funguses.** To read about the funguses of the forest, TURN TO PAGE 20.

... **fruit and leaves from trees.** To read about the trees of the forest, TURN TO PAGE 34.

... **green mountain bamboo.** To read about green mountain bamboo, TURN TO PAGE 56.

MARTIAL EAGLE *(Polemaetus bellicosus)*

The martial eagle soars over the rain forest. Her wings stretch out to nearly 7 feet (2 meters). She is the largest eagle in Africa. But right now, she's flying so high up in the sky that you would need binoculars to see her.

She tips her wings and soars lower. She skirts the edge of the **canopy** now. Only her shadow alerts the treetop animals that she is above. Her sharp eyes are on the lookout for a snack. She can pick a bird off a branch or spot a hare on the forest floor.

In a blink, she pulls her wings in and drops down through the branches. She's spied dinner. Her sharp talons (claws) reach out and nab a young monkey right from its screaming family.

As they fly away, the monkey wriggles. Uh-oh. Her talons didn't kill the monkey, and he's fighting back. Suddenly, she's in big trouble. The monkey grabs at her feathers. She loses control, and they tumble to the forest floor. As they hit the ground, she releases him. She has to. If he pulled out her feathers or hurt her wings, she wouldn't be able to fly. And if she can't fly, she'll die.

Immediately, the monkey scrambles back up the tree to his family. The eagle fluffs out her feathers to see how much damage the monkey did. Then she takes off on another hunt.

Last night for dinner, the martial eagle gulped down . . .

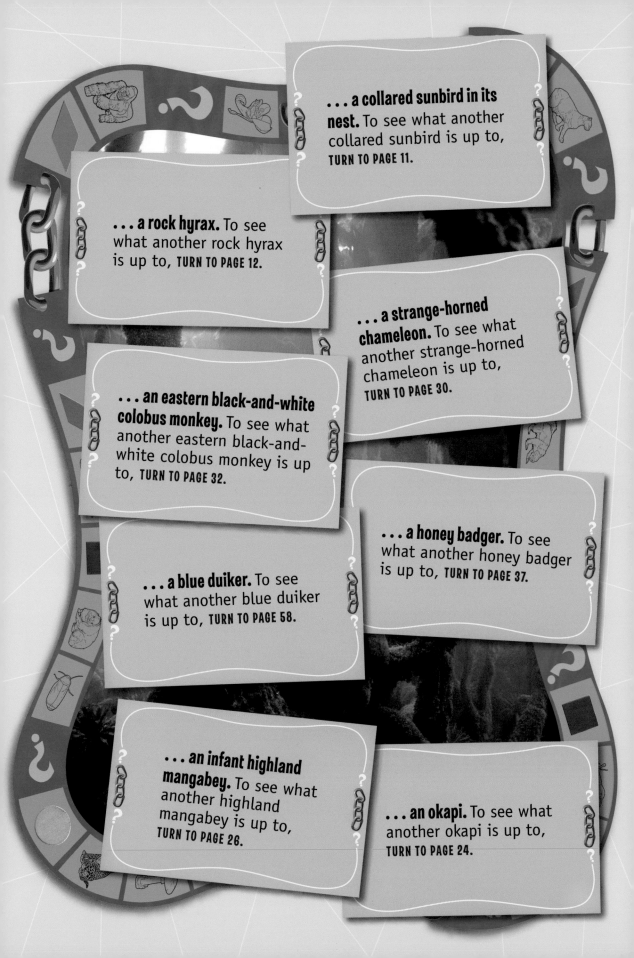

. . . a collared sunbird in its nest. To see what another collared sunbird is up to, TURN TO PAGE 11.

. . . a rock hyrax. To see what another rock hyrax is up to, TURN TO PAGE 12.

. . . a strange-horned chameleon. To see what another strange-horned chameleon is up to, TURN TO PAGE 30.

. . . an eastern black-and-white colobus monkey. To see what another eastern black-and-white colobus monkey is up to, TURN TO PAGE 32.

. . . a honey badger. To see what another honey badger is up to, TURN TO PAGE 37.

. . . a blue duiker. To see what another blue duiker is up to, TURN TO PAGE 58.

. . . an infant highland mangabey. To see what another highland mangabey is up to, TURN TO PAGE 26.

. . . an okapi. To see what another okapi is up to, TURN TO PAGE 24.

RUWENZORI TURACO

(Ruwenzorornis johnstoni)

The Ruwenzori turaco flaps her rounded wings and jumps from one branch down to the next. She's not a strong flyer, so jumping or walking is often easier. Her mate sees her approaching. He's been warming their eggs while she's out searching for fruit for breakfast.

She settles on the flimsy nest built of sticks. Then she sits on their three eggs. Her mate bustles off for his meal. His long tail drags behind him as he walks down the branch. Turacos can actually change the direction of one of their toes. When they are perched on a branch, they usually have three toes forward and one to the back. But when they walk, they can move another toe to the back. That gives them better balance.

The female waits. Not long after her mate leaves, she feels the telltale nudging from under her. Her eggs are hatching! When her mate returns to the nest, three fuzzy, black baby turacos greet him. They won't get the vibrant green, red, blue, and purple colors of their parents' feathers until later. The two parents will spend the next three weeks feeding and protecting their chicks.

Last night for dinner, the Ruwenzori turaco pecked at . . .

Seed Spreader

Because Ruwenzori turacos eat so much fruit, they play a very important role in the African cloud forest. They eat a lot of fruit, but their bodies don't digest all of it. The parts that aren't digested, such as the seeds, are pooped out. Plants and trees depend on animals such as the turacos to spread seeds to new places to grow. So as Ruwenzori turacos walk around and poop in the cloud forest, they are also planting the seeds for the fruit trees of the future.

. . . **flowers, such as impatiens and begonias.** To read about impatiens and begonias, TURN TO PAGE 22.

. . . **a swallowtail butterfly.** To see what another butterfly is up to, TURN TO PAGE 27.

. . . **fruit and leaves from trees.** To read about the trees of the forest, TURN TO PAGE 34.

. . . **green mountain bamboo.** To read about green mountain bamboo, TURN TO PAGE 56.

. . . **termites.** To see what other termites are up to, TURN TO PAGE 47.

. . . **a speckled cockroach.** To see what another speckled cockroach is up to, TURN TO PAGE 14.

GIANT OTTER SHREW *(Potamogale velox)*

Splash! The giant otter shrew pops her head out of the mountain stream. She propels herself through the water with her wide tail. She swishes it back and forth in the water the way a fish uses its tail. Her legs are tucked tight against her sides. Her bristly nose is barely above the water.

She dives down. Flaps on her nostrils keep water out of her nose. Underwater, she glides. A frog darts out of the way near the surface. The stiff whiskers on her face sense his movement. In a couple of quick bites, the frog becomes her dinner.

She takes a breath again. The sun is coming up. It is time to head back to the den. She swims to the bank of the stream. At its edge, she ducks down. The entrance to her den is underwater. She comes up in a hollow dug under the stream bank. It's warm and cozy there, lined with dry leaves. It's just right for taking a rest while the daytime animals of the forest begin to wake up.

Last night for dinner, the giant otter shrew headed upstream by land. She trapped and swallowed . . .

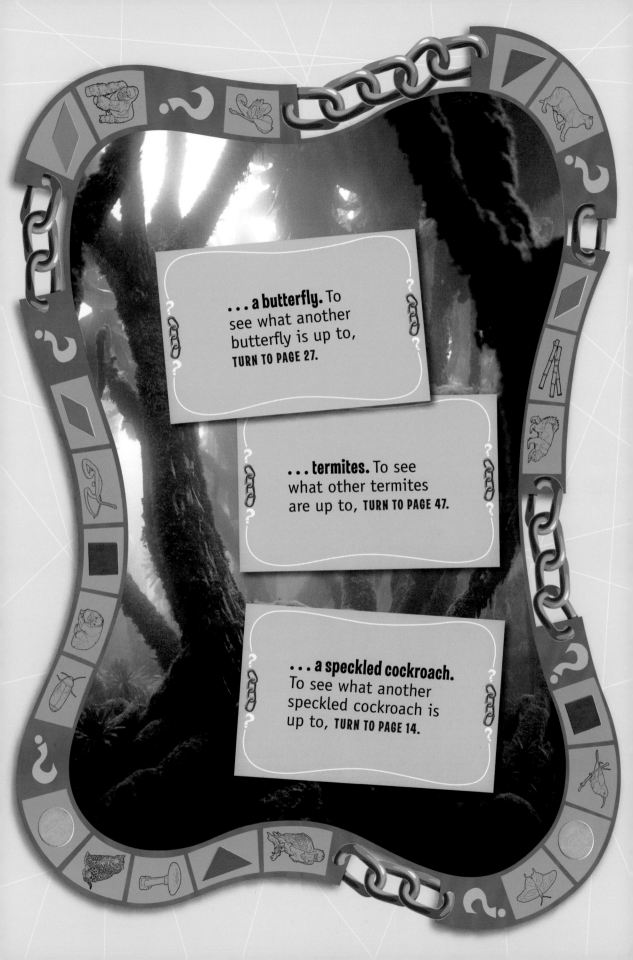

. . . a butterfly. To see what another butterfly is up to, TURN TO PAGE 27.

. . . termites. To see what other termites are up to, TURN TO PAGE 47.

. . . a speckled cockroach. To see what another speckled cockroach is up to, TURN TO PAGE 14.

GREEN MOUNTAIN BAMBOO *(Arundinaria alpina)*

The green mountain bamboo almost grows right before your eyes. Bamboo is the fastest-growing woody plant in the world. It tangles and weaves so thickly that it is impossible to walk through the African cloud forest. This shelter creates the perfect hiding place for the creatures of the forest. It also keeps intruders out. When people need to travel through the forest, they have to hack a path through the dense branches with a large knife called a machete.

The roots of green mountain bamboo soak up nutrients in the soil that were left behind by decomposers and the **decomposing** bodies of dead animals. *Last night for dinner, the bamboo soaked up nutrients from . . .*

Forest Foundation

Bamboo is more than just food and shelter in the forest. Its shoots are so strong that they are used to support concrete. But in the African cloud forest, bamboo's real strength is underground. A bamboo tree's wide roots keep the soil on steep hills from eroding, or sliding away. By stopping erosion, bamboo helps keep other forest plants healthy.

. . . termites. To see what other termites are up to, TURN TO PAGE 47.

. . . a dead martial eagle. To see what another martial eagle is up to, TURN TO PAGE 49.

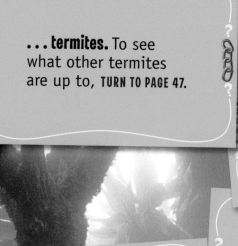

. . . a dead leopard. To see what another leopard is up to, TURN TO PAGE 8.

. . . a dead chimpanzee. To see what another chimpanzee is up to, TURN TO PAGE 44.

. . . a dead African golden cat. To see what another African golden cat is up to, TURN TO PAGE 28.

. . . a dead strange-horned chameleon. To see what another strange-horned chameleon is up to, TURN TO PAGE 30.

. . . a dead giant forest hog. To see what another giant forest hog is up to, TURN TO PAGE 16.

. . . a dead black mamba. To see what another black mamba is up to, TURN TO PAGE 40.

BLUE DUIKER
(Cephalophus monticola)

The blue duiker pair steps out into the cool night. The male waits while the female licks and grooms his head. Two tiny horns stick out of the top of his head. Everything about the blue duikers is tiny. They stand just 20 inches (51 centimeters) tall. But their small size helps them to get around the thick brush and bamboo of the forest. A bigger antelope would get tangled and be slow and noisy.

The pair patrols their territory. Now and then, they stop to chomp down a piece of fruit dropped from above by a monkey. At the edges of their territory, they rub their faces on the trunks of the trees. They have scent glands under their eyes. Rubbing their faces on trees releases the scent. The duikers use the scent and their dung (poop) to mark their territory.

58

Cause and Effect

Blue duikers are fairly common in the forest. But they could be in trouble in the future. Blue duikers depend on the fruit that monkeys drop from the trees. The problem is that monkeys are disappearing from the forest. If there are fewer or no monkeys up above, there's less food for the blue duiker. And that means fewer blue duikers.

The female pauses for a drink. Blue duikers don't need much water, but she takes a moment to lick some moisture off a shrub's leaves. Meanwhile, the male's white tail bobs ahead. She can tell by the way it moves that he's found something. She trots along to catch up. He's killed a rat. They both pull and chew on it. Blue duikers are the only antelopes that eat meat. *Last night for dinner, the blue duiker munched on . . .*

. . . a collared sunbird that has fallen out of its nest. To see what another collared sunbird is up to, TURN TO PAGE 11.

. . . flowers, such as impatiens and begonias. To read about impatiens and begonias, TURN TO PAGE 22.

. . . Ruwenzori turaco eggs. To see what another Ruwenzori turaco is up to, TURN TO PAGE 52.

. . . fruit and leaves from trees. To read about the trees of the forest, TURN TO PAGE 34.

. . . a diadem butterfly. To see what another butterfly is up to, TURN TO PAGE 27.

. . . mushrooms and other funguses. To read about the funguses of the forest, TURN TO PAGE 20.

. . . a speckled cockroach. To see what another speckled cockroach is up to, TURN TO PAGE 14.

. . . green mountain bamboo. To read about green mountain bamboo, TURN TO PAGE 56.

GLOSSARY

brachiating: swinging (as from branch to branch) using the arms

canopy: the highest branchy layer of a forest formed by the treetops

carnivore: an animal that eats other animals

colony: a mass of plants or animals of one species that live together

decomposers: living things, such as insects, that feed on dead plants and animals

decomposing: decaying, or breaking down, after dying

endangered: close to dying out

epiphytes: plants that don't need soil to grow. Epiphytes grow against other plants but get water and nutrients from the air and rain.

extinct: no longer existing

food chain: a system in which energy is transferred from plants to animals as each eats and is eaten

food web: many food chains linked together

habitat: an area where a group of plants or animals naturally lives and grows

nutrients: substances, especially in food, that help a plant or animal survive

poachers: people who steal or kill wild animals illegally

predators: animals that hunt and kill other animals for food

prey: animals that are hunted for food by other animals

primary consumers: animals that eat plants

producers: living things that make their own food. Plants are producers. They draw nutrients from soil and use energy from the sun to create their own food from water and carbon dioxide.

rain forest: a thick forest that normally gets more than 160 inches (406 centimeters) of rain a year

secondary consumers: small animals and insects that eat other animals and insects

species: a group of related animals or plants

tertiary consumers: animals that hunt other animals for food and that have few natural enemies

troop: a group of animals, such as chimpanzees, living together

venom: poison used by snakes to defend themselves and to catch food

FURTHER READING AND WEBSITES

BOOKS

Collard, Sneed, III. *The Forest in the Clouds*. Watertown, MA: Charlesbridge, 2000. Africa is not the only place with cloud forests. Read about the cloud forest in Costa Rica in this book.

Goodall, Jane. *The Chimpanzees I Love: Saving Their World and Ours*. New York: Scholastic, 2001. Famous chimpanzee expert Jane Goodall shares what she's learned about these endangered animals through her life's work.

Matthews, Tom. *Light Shining Through the Mists: A Photobiography of Dian Fossey*. Washington, D.C.: National Geographic Children's Books, 1998. Beautiful photographs highlight scientist Dian Fossey's study of gorillas in Rwanda.

Pimm, Nancy Roe. *The Heart of the Beast*. Plain City, OH: Darby Creek, 2007. Pimm tells the stories of eight well-known gorillas, with information on gorilla behavior, diet, and development.

Turner, Pamela S. *Gorilla Doctors: Saving Endangered Great Apes*. New York: Houghton Mifflin, 2005. This book profiles the Mountain Gorilla Veterinary Project (MGVP) and its work to save endangered gorillas.

Welsbacher, Anne. *Protecting the Earth's Rain Forests*. Minneapolis: Lerner Publications Company, 2009. Part of the Saving Our Living Earth series, this book looks at the problems facing the world's rain forests and how we can help stop the damage.

WEBSITES

Africa: Explore the Regions
http://www.pbs.org/wnet/africa/explore/rainforest/rainforest_overview_lo.html
This PBS website explores Africa's rain forests—the people, cultures, animals, and plant life.

African Wildlife Foundation
http://www.awf.org/section/wildlife/gallery
Learn about the size, habitats, and behavior—even hear the calls and sounds—of cloud forest and other African animals.

National Geographic Kids
http://kids.nationalgeographic.com/Animals/CreatureFeature
Many of the African cloud forest animals are profiled with photos, videos, maps, and links.

SELECTED BIBLIOGRAPHY

Africanfauna.com. 2004. http://www.africanfauna.com (April 14, 2008).

Burnie, David. *Animal: The Definitive Visual Guide to the World's Wildlife*. New York: DK, 2005.

Dudley, Joseph P., and Mark McGinley. "East African Montane Forests." *The Encyclopedia of Earth*. 2008. http://www.eoearth.org/article/East_African _montane_forests (April 14, 2008).

IUCN. "2007 IUCN Red List of Threatened Species." *The IUCN Species Survival Commission*. N.d. http://www.iucnredlist.org/ (April 14, 2008).

National Audubon Society. *National Audubon Society Field Guide to African Wildlife*. New York: Alfred A. Knopf. 1995.

Pandolfi, Massimo. *Equatorial Africa*. Milwaukee: Raintree, 1989.

Plumptre, Andrew, et al. "Albertine Rift." *Hotspots Revisited*. 2004. http:// www.biodiversityscience.org/publications/hotspots/AlbertineRift.html (April 14, 2008).

University of Michigan. *Animal Diversity Web*. 1995–2008. http:// animaldiversity.ummz.umich.edu/site/index.html (February 20, 2008).

World Wildlife Fund. "Albertine Rift Montane Forest Ecoregion." *worldwildlife .org*. 2007. http://www.panda.org/about_wwf/where_we_work/africa/ solutions_by_region/eastern_africa/our_solutions/albertine_rift_forest_/ index.cfm (April 14, 2008).

———. "Wildfinder." *worldwildlife.org*. 2008. http://www.worldwildlife.org/ wildfinder/ (April 14, 2008).

INDEX

African golden cat (*Felis aurata*), 28

begonias, 22
black mamba (*Dendroaspis polyleptis*), 40–41
blue duiker (*Cephalophus monticola*), 58
butterflies, 27
Bwindi National Park (Uganda), 35

chimpanzee (*Pan troglodytes*), 4, 44–46
cloud forest: climate of, 4; destruction of, 19, 26, 34, 46; map of, 5
collared sunbird (*Anthreptes collaris*), 11
consumers, definitions of: primary consumer, 6; secondary consumer, 6; tertiary consumer, 6

decomposers, 6, 14, 20, 22, 47

eastern black-and-white colobus (*Colobus guereza*), 32
epiphytes, 34

food web (diagram), 31
fungus, 20

giant forest hog (*Hylochoerus meinertzhageni*), 14, 16
giant otter shrew (*Potamogale velox*), 54
green mountain bamboo (*Arundinaria alpina*), 4, 6, 56

highland mangabey (*Lophocebus kipunji*), 26

honey badger (*Mellivora capensis*), 8–9, 37–38
humans: and deforestation, 19, 26, 34, 46; and hunting, 19, 24, 30, 44, 46; other negative effects of, 27, 46; positive effects of, 46

impatiens, 22

leopard (*Panthera pardus*), 8–9, 32, 33

martial eagle (*Polemaetus bellicosus*), 49
mountain gorilla (*Gorilla beringei beringei*), 4, 6, 18–19

okapi (*Okapi johnstoni*), 24, 25

photosynthesis (diagram), 34
plants of the cloud forest, 4, 11, 30, 34, 56
producers, definition of, 6

rock hyrax (*Procavia capensis*), 12, 41
Rwenzori Mountains, 30
Ruwenzori turaco (*Ruwenzorornis johnstoni*), 52

speckled cockroach (*Nauphoeta cinerea*), 6, 14
strange-horned chameleon (*Bradypodion xenorhinia*), 30

termites (*Macrotermes vitrialatus*), 40, 44, 47, 48
trees, 4, 34, 56
tropical house gecko (*Hemidactylus mabouia*), 43

63

Photo Acknowledgments

The images in this book are used with the permission of: © Michael Nichols/National Geographic/Getty Images, background photographs on pp. 1, 10, 13, 15, 17, 21, 23, 25, 29, 33, 36, 39, 42, 48, 51, 53, 55, 57, 59; © age fotostock/SuperStock, pp. 4–5, 6–7; © Anup Shah/Photodisc/Getty Images, p. 8; © Joseph Van Os/Riser/Getty Images, p. 9; © Adam Jones/Photodisc/Getty Images, p. 11; © Manoj Shah/Riser/Getty Images, p. 12; © Dr. James L. Castner/Visuals Unlimited, Inc., p. 14; © Penny Boyd/Alamy, p. 16; © Mauritius/SuperStock, pp. 18, 24 (bottom), 46; © Joe McDonald/Visuals Unlimited, Inc., pp. 19, 50; © Patricio Robles Gil/Minden Pictures, p. 20 (inset); © Frans Lanting/CORBIS, p. 20 (main); © Francois Merlet/FLPA, p. 22 (top); © Chris Demetriou/FLPA, p. 22 (bottom); © Ken Lucas/Visuals Unlimited, Inc., p. 24 (top); © Tim Davenport, p. 26; © PATTI MURRAY/Animals Animals, p. 27; © Art Wolfe/www.ArtWolfe.com, p. 28; © Ingo Arndt/naturepl.com, p. 30 (top); © Bruce Davidson/naturepl.com, p. 30 (bottom); © Gerry Ellis/Minden Pictures, p. 32; © Staffan Widstrand/naturepl.com, p. 34; © Adrian Bailey/Aurora/Getty Images, p. 35; © LEE LYON/SURVIVAL/OSF/Animals Animals, p. 37; © Francois Savigny/naturepl.com, p. 38; © Photocyclops.com/SuperStock, p. 40; © Cagan Sekercioglu/Visuals Unlimited, Inc., p. 41; © Pete Oxford/DRK PHOTO, p. 43; © Daryl Balfour/The Image Bank/Getty Images, p. 45; © Nick Greaves/Alamy, p. 47 (bottom); © Cyril Ruoso/Minden Pictures, p. 47 (top); © Shin Yoshino/Minden Pictures, p. 49; © Nik Borrow, p. 52; Photo by Carlton Ward Jr/Smithsonian Institution CCES, p. 54; © Peter Davey/FLPA, p. 56; © Arco Images GmbH/Alamy, p. 58. Illustrations for game board and pieces © Bill Hauser/Independent Picture Service.

Front cover: © Michael Nichols/National Geographic/Getty Images (background); © Tim Laman/National Geographic/Getty Images (left); © Peter Davey/FLPA (second from left); © George Grall/National Geographic/Getty Images (second from right); © Annie Katz/Photographer's Choice/Getty Images (right).

About the Authors

Don Wojahn and Becky Wojahn are school library media specialists by day and writers by night. Their natural habitat is the temperate forests of northwestern Wisconsin, where they share their den with two animal-loving sons and two big black dogs. The Wojahns are the authors of all twelve books in the Follow that Food Chain series.